Poem of the Week

Seasonal Poems Phonics, Too!

Betsy Franco

A Teaching Resource Center Publication

W9-DCA-994

Published by
Teaching Resource Center
14525 SW Millikan, #11910 Beaverton, OR 97005-2343
1-800-833-3389
www.trcabc.com

Edited by Anne Linehan and Laura Woodard
Design and production by Janis Poe
Illustrations by Linda Starr

Printed in the United States of America
ISBN: 1-56785-039-1

Acknowledgements

For Davy, who helps me iron out
the kinks in my poetry.

Thank you to the following teachers, and the
children in their classes, who chanted, illustrated,
and interacted with my poems:

Diane McCoy
Denise Dauler
Serena Chandley
Annette Isaacson

Thank you, as well, to the children
at El Carmelo School who gave me ideas for
the poems by just being themselves.

Choosing Poems

You're free to use the poems in any order that suits you. Even if you're on a year-round schedule, you're set. To help you appreciate the versatility of the collection, the poems have been organized in two ways:

1. In the table of contents, the seasonal poems come first. Following the seasonal poems is a set of poems appropriate for any time of year.

2. In the chart on page 3, the poems have been organized by phonemes, and those phonemes are spelled out in the chart. All the poems in the collection are included, and seasonal poems in the list are starred for easy identification.

Table of Contents

Poem of the Week by Phoneme

*seasonal poems

Teacher Notes

Use *Poem of the Week* to share the rhythm and cadence of poetry and the joy of poetic language with the children in your class. The topics of the poems were chosen to reflect a child's world, making this book a natural, weekly link to the family. And if you choose, you can use each poem as the context for raising phonemic awareness and inspiring creativity.

Overview

Poetry is a mainstay in the primary classroom. But it's usually up to you to beg, steal, or borrow the poems you need. It's usually your job to find poetry that's relevant, lively, touching, and thematically appropriate.

Relax. The poems are written. The themes are in place. There's one poem per week, including a special set of seasonal poems. There's an extra bonus, too. Since phonemic awareness is coming into such sharp focus, each poem highlights a particular phoneme.

If you choose to, you can follow the suggestions that accompany each poem. That way, you can enjoy the poetry with your children, while at the same time introducing, teaching, or reviewing the appropriate phonemes. The suggestions will help you make the poems interactive as well.

Along with the poems and suggestions, we've provided strips for each poem that fit into the Desktop Pocket Chart. With all these tools, groups can enjoy the poems, individual children can learn from and elaborate on the poems, and you can relax and enjoy your teaching.

Versatility Plus

You can choose poems by:
    theme
    season
    week
    phonemic focus
    your particular interests

What You've Got

- A poem for every week of the year
- A set of thematic poems for each season
- Suggestions on how to bring out the specific phonemic focus of each poem
- Suggestions for making the poems personal and interactive for the children
- Poetry strips and an illustration that fit into the Desktop Pocket Chart

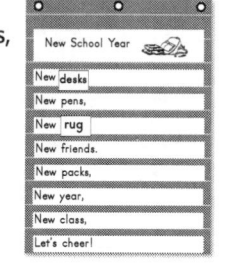

12"wide x 16"high,
10 pockets

Student Poems

For every week of the year, you have a poem, enlarged for easy reading. You can make a copy of the poem for each child, leaving off the Suggestions for Going Further.

Strips for the Desktop Pocket Chart

You're all set for group work. By copying and cutting out the enlarged strips (starting on page 56) on index tag and using them in the Desktop Pocket Chart, you can display a poem for many eyes to see. Groups of children can interact with the poem using this intimate, yet practical medium.

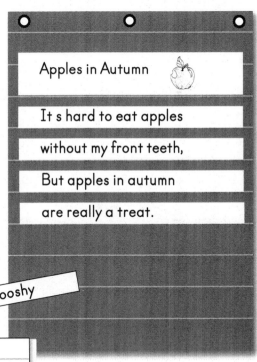

ee, ea

Suggestions for Going Further

1. Make word cards from the long e words in the poem that contain the vowel pattern ea or ee. Encourage children to sort the words in different ways; for example, they could sort by vowel pattern, by location of the vowel pattern in the word, or by the number of letters in the word.
2. Let children use the following frame to change the fruit and/or the season. For example, they could use peaches or cherries in summer.
    It's hard to eat ____
    without my front teeth.
    But ____ in ____
    are really a treat.
3. Talk about what happens to apples that fall to the ground. On the Desktop Pocket Chart, put a sticky note over the word squooshy in line 5, and write in other possible adjectives that the children think of to replace it.

17

Apples in Autumn

It's hard to eat apples
without my front teeth,
But apples in autumn
are really a treat.
The apples are squooshy
down under my feet,
But those from the tree
are still crunchy and sweet!

Suggestions for Going Further

The suggestions next to the poems are your easy-to-use guides for extending the poems, if the ideas suit your needs. The suggestions point out the hidden phonemic treasures in the poems and how to make use of them. The suggestions also include ideas for extending the poems and making them interactive and personal for the children.

Included among the student poems are twenty-two seasonal poems which are perfect for monthly calendar work. The poems capture the essence of each season.

There are many ways to use *Poem of the Week*. You can copy the student poems for individual use. You can reconstruct the poem on a Desktop Pocket Chart for group work. You can make your own strips for a Standard Pocket Chart.

Ways to Use the Student Poems

- Read through and select the poem that suits your needs.
- Fill in any blanks or add blanks to the poem, if you choose.
- Make a copy of the poem without the Suggestions. Or cut out the poem and adhere it to the center of another paper before copying.
- Enjoy the poem for the beauty of the words, the rhythm, and the content.
- Have each child add the poem to a personal poetry anthology.
- Follow the Suggestions for Going Further that make sense to you.
- Send poem books home to be shared with family members.

Going Further with the Student Poems

‹ Make the poems interactive. Give children a chance to personalize the poem by creating a blank for them to fill with their own words. It's as simple as whiting out or taping over a word or phrase in the student poems before making copies.

‹ Let children answer questions posed in the poems. Here is an example of an Interview Form to go with You are Special on page 15.

Our Garden

We plow with our shovels,
Now time to plant seeds.
_____ for us,
and flowers for bees.
When rows are all planted,
we'll make a scarecrow
to keep out the birds
so our garden can grow.

Interview Form

What is your name?
Eduardo

What is your favorite game?
football

What do you like?
playing with my dog

What can you do really well?
Stand on my head

What can you teach us that is silly or new? a joke

Interviewed by: Kelsey

Edgardo
Nice and Friendly

I say hi to Rosa,
Rosa says hi to Lan,
Lan says hi to Bo,
and Bo says hi to Don.
When I feel nice and friendly,
I like to pass it on.

Mom says hi to dad

› Let children illustrate
the poem or make an
appropriate border
for it.

⌃ Have children highlight
or underline the partic-
ular phoneme featured
in the poem.

‹ Add new verses or
write variations on the
poem using poetry
frames.

⌃ Make the poems into
word problems.

The pup sees Jelly _____,
The pup falls down.
The pup has turned
from white to Purple _____.

Lunch

I <u>crunch</u>, I <u>munch</u>.
I <u>chew</u> a <u>bunch</u> of carrots
when I eat my <u>lunch</u>.

And when I've <u>munched</u>
on all my <u>lunch</u>,
I wash it down
with cold fruit <u>punch</u>.

So what's to <u>munch</u>
inside your <u>lunch</u>?

Name Maya

<u>50</u> ¢ each

We sold 4 cakes.
We sold 2 lemonades.
We made 2.50.

lemonade and
cakes
comeing rite up

My Dream

I __ailed a __eaf,
I __ailed to __ea.
I ate a hot __eal
of oat __eal and __ea.
I painted a sun __eam,
I __ __ained a small __ __ea.
The __ __am that I __ __eamed
seemed as __eal as could be.

› White out or tape over
onsets or rimes in the
poem, and let children
fill them in.

‹ Make lists of rhyming
words from the poem.
Or make webs of words
that share a phonemic
element or rime that is
emphasized in the
poem.

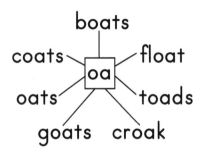

boats
coats — oa — float
oats — toads
goats   croak

Ways to Use the Desktop Pocket Chart

- Copy the poetry strips and the illustration onto index tag.
- Cut out the strips and the illustration.
- Reconstruct the poem in the Desktop Pocket Chart using the poetry strips. We've numbered each line to minimize confusion. You can keep the numbers or cut them off. If a poem has 10 lines, the title has been designed to fit behind the first line in the top pocket.
- Gather a group of children to recite the poem together and enjoy its rhythm.
- Work with the poem's phonemic focus in a relevant context.

Going Further with the Desktop Pocket Chart

- Use non-permanent markers, Wikki Stix, or highlighting tape to highlight phonemes on the pocket chart strips.
- Let children use a pointer such as a Magic Wand to identify particular phonemes or rhyming words.

- Use sticky notes to cover words in the poem. Let children suggest new words to write in their place to personalize or change the poem. Alternatively, you can use blank word cards made from heavy paper to cover and replace words. (Cards should be about 2" long, 1" high.)

- Cover phrases in the poem with blank strips and let children interact with the poem by rewriting the phrases. (Strips should be about 1" high.)

When youre running through the sprinkler,

there are lots of games to play,

You can

or run every-which-way.

pick up the sprinkler,

One Hundred

One hundred b<u>oa</u>ts

fl<u>oa</u>t on the sea,

One hundred t<u>oa</u>ds

cr<u>oa</u>k by the tree,

One hundred g<u>oa</u>ts

eat lots of <u>oa</u>ts,

How many raindrops

on our <u>oa</u>ts?

New School Year

New desks

New pens,

New rug

New friends.

New packs,

New year,

New class,

Let's cheer!

Have children use letters to build banks of words that share the same phoneme as the one featured in the poem.

Use chart paper to create banks or webs of words with the same phonemic element as the poem.

Make word cards focusing on a phoneme from the poem, and let children sort the cards in different ways.

| mess | best | get |
| dress | vest | set |

Magic Wand Pattern

Copy the wand onto tagboard and cut it out.
Trace the wand pattern onto cardboard and cut it out.
Glue the tagboard wand to the cardboard wand.
Decorate the wand with colored markers, sequins, ribbons, and glitter.

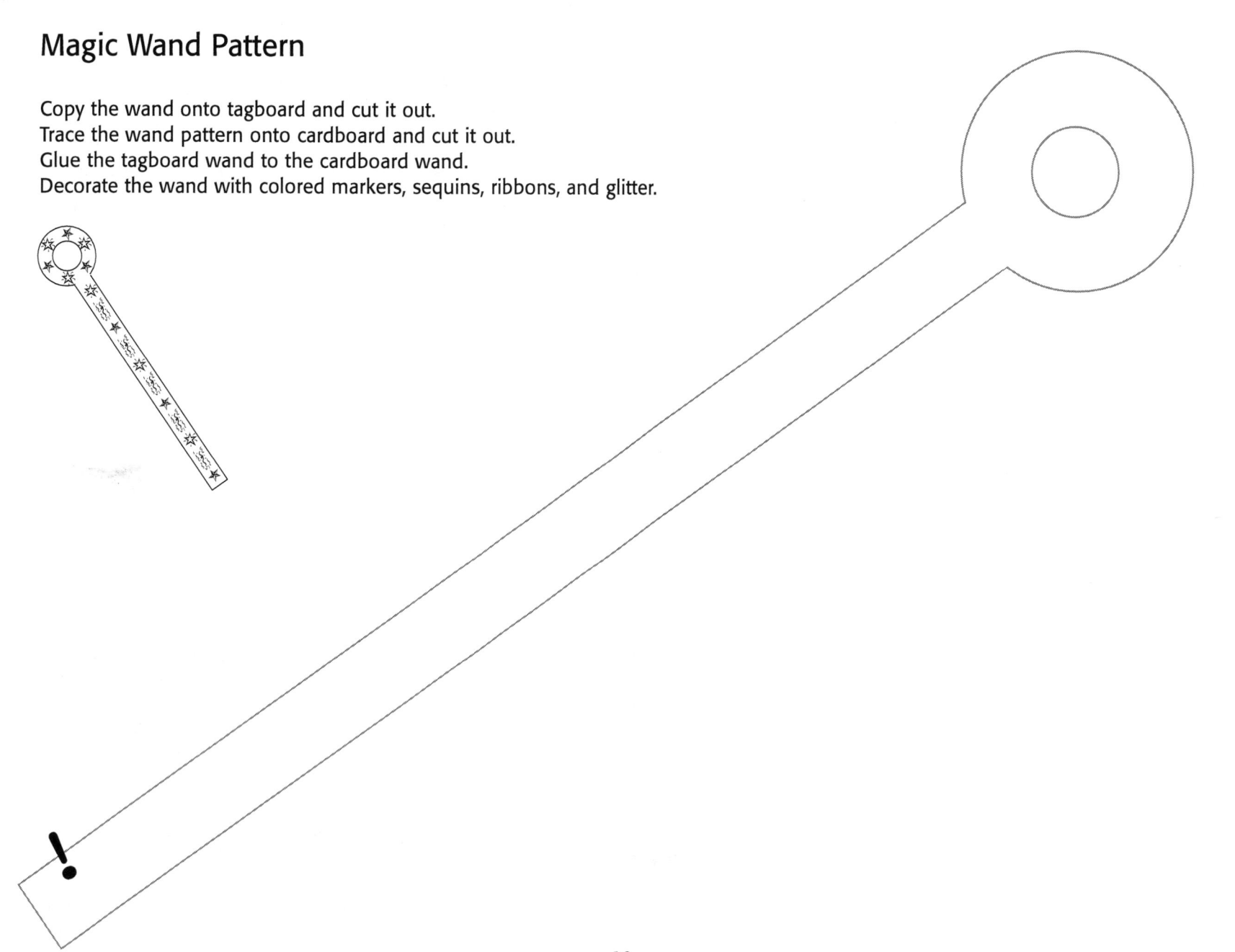

Suggestions for Going Further

1. Brainstorm and record a list of all the new things that come with a new school year. Before copying the student poem, consider taping over or whiting out some of the non-rhyming words such as *books* and *packs* and replacing them with a blank. That way, the children can personalize the poem. Alternatively, you could do this on the poetry strips (pages 58-59) by replacing the same words, *books* and *packs*, with blank word cards (2" x 1") or sticky notes, and writing in children's suggestions.

2. Have fun with initial consonants. What letter is used to start words the most? (N for *New*) How many times? (8) What letter is repeated twice? (*p* for *pens*, *packs*) What other beginning sounds do you hear and see? (*b* for *books*, *r* for *room*, *y* for *year*) Note that *b*, *p*, and *r* are among the most frequently used consonants. *Friends*, *class*, and *cheer* have initial blends and digraphs.

New School Year

New room,
New pens,
New books,
New friends.
New packs,
New year,
New class,
Let's cheer!

initial consonants

Suggestions for Going Further

Note: *Lan*, a Vietnamese name, is pronounced *lahn*.

1. This poem lends itself to a friendly "Pass it On" activity. After placing the poem in the Desktop Pocket Chart, cut out and insert the line "____says hi to ____" in the last line of the chart. Have children sit in a circle. Use name cards that fit in the chart (2" x 1"), or sticky notes, with the children's names on them. Arrange the names in the order the children are sitting. Slip the first two names into the blanks. Have everyone read the line. Then have the first child say hi to the second. Place the second child's name in blank one and the third child's name in blank two. Continue on:

First round:	Tom says hi to Kwaku.
Second round:	Kwaku says hi to Maria.
Third round:	Maria says hi to Sue. etc.

2. When children are reading each other's names, focus on the initial consonants of the names.

Nice and Friendly

I say hi to Rosa,
Rosa says hi to Lan,
Lan says hi to Bo,
and Bo says hi to Don.
When I feel nice and friendly,
I like to pass it on.

_____ says hi to _____.

Suggestions for Going Further

1. Lead a discussion about how children can make friends by being friendly. Have children draw pictures of themselves playing with a friend, or potential friend, in the class. Perhaps each child could name the friend in their picture and show the picture to the other child.
2. Let children use a pointer such as a Magic Wand to point to all the long *e* words in the poem. The long *e* words can be divided into two groups, those with *e* and those with *ee*. As you record them, let the children decide which group each word belongs in.

13

We All Need Friends

"Hi," "Hello,"
"Come play with me."
These are friendly words, you see.
To be a friend
can take awhile,
yet it can start with just a smile.
I need a friend
to play with me.
I'll be your friend if you agree.

Suggestions for Going Further

1. Consider cutting off the word *bus* in line 1 of the poetry strips and letting children take turns personalizing the poem. Children can write their modes of transportation on word cards made of heavy paper (2″ long by 1″ high) and insert their cards in the Desktop Pocket Chart. These same cards can be used to create a Coming to School graph.
2. Let children make a mural showing all the ways they come to school. Children can include themselves in the picture. Details from the poem can also be used.
3. Use a pointer such as a Magic Wand to point to all the long *i* words in the Desktop Pocket Chart poem. You can even highlight the words with markers, Wikki Stix, or highlighting tape. Then let children use sets of letters to build words with the following rimes: *ike, ive, ide.* The Word Builder Kit works well for this.

Coming to School

I come by bus,
Mike comes by trike.
Some people drive,
and some people hike.
Spike likes to run,
Ike likes to bike.
The ways that we come
aren't always alike.

Suggestions for Going Further

1. After reading this self-esteem poem, you can do some beginning consonant work by grouping, and even graphing, children's names by initial consonants. For older children, names can be grouped by first or last names or by final consonants. An alphabetized class directory can also be made.
2. Have children take turns reciting things they like (food, animals, activities, colors) that begin with the same letter as their names. (E.g., Davy likes dogs.) Children can write and illustrate these sentences about themselves.
3. Children can also write the answer to the questions in the poem on their student poem sheets. Or they can pair up and interview each other, using the poem questions.

   Note: Since this poem has more lines than the Desktop Pocket Chart, the title strip has been designed to fit behind the first line.

15

You are Special

What is your name
and your favorite game?
What do you like
and what can you do?
What can you teach us
that's silly or new?
So many things
we wish that we knew.
Yet what makes you special
is just being you.

Suggestions for Going Further

1. Read through the poem, line by line, looking for short vowel sounds. They are all represented. (A: *has, cannot*) (E: *legs, red*) (I: *in, it*) (O: *cannot*) (U: *but, run*).
2. Discuss the fact that trees are given human qualities in the poem. Have children draw a picture of the poem in a way that reflects this.
3. Let children write a poem about the human qualities of leaves. (The poem could start as follows: "A leaf has fingers" or "A leaf has veins").

A Tree Has Arms

A tree has arms
but has no legs,
It cannot run around.
But in the fall,
it wears a gown
of yellow, orange,
and brown.

Suggestions for Going Further

1. Make word cards from the long *e* words in the poem that contain the vowel pattern *ea* or *ee*. Encourage children to sort the words in different ways; for example, they could sort by vowel pattern, by location of the vowel pattern in the word, or by the number of letters in the word.

2. Let children use the following frame to change the fruit and/or the season. For example, they could use peaches or cherries in summer.

    It's hard to eat _____
    without my front teeth.
    But _____ in _____
    are really a treat.

3. Talk about what happens to apples that fall to the ground. On the Desktop Pocket Chart, put a sticky note over the word *squooshy* in line 5, and write in other adjectives that the children think of to replace it.

17

Apples in Autumn

It's hard to eat apples
without my front teeth,
But apples in autumn
are really a treat.
The apples are squooshy
down under my feet,
But those from the tree
are still crunchy and sweet!

Suggestions for Going Further

1. If you white out or tape over the word *white* in the student poems, then children can personalize the poem by writing in the true color of their backpacks. These colors can be graphed as well.
2. Let children use a pointer such as a Magic Wand to point to all the *ck* words in the poem. These words can be highlighted with markers on the student poems and with markers, Wikki Stix, or highlighting tape on the Desktop Pocket Chart. Help children notice that the *ck* always appears at the end or the middle of words. Go one step further by having children brainstorm a list of words that rhyme with *back*.
3. Take advantage of the opposites in the poem by having children generate a list of more opposites that might describe a backpack. (*new/old, big/small, dirty/clean, torn/mended, open/closed, stuffed/empty*).

Lists of opposites having nothing to do with backpacks can also be recorded.

Backpacks

My backpack is white,
Your backpack is black.
My backpack's so full,
it's hard to unpack.
Your backpack is heavy,
My backpack is light.
It's smack on my back,
It rides piggyback.

Suggestions for Going Further

1. Have children do careful detective work to find all the words with *ng* or *nk* in the poem. On the Desktop Pocket Chart, highlight the words using markers, Wikki Stix, or highlighting tape. Then write the rimes *ank, ink, ing,* and *ong* on chart paper, and use them to generate banks of rhyming words.

2. Have children personalize the poem by completing the frame:

   Thanks for _____,
   Thanks for _____,
   Thank you, I think, for _____.

Note that this poem can be used for self-esteem. Children can give thanks for their abilities, their personality traits, and other things that make them unique.

I'm Thankful

Thanks for my tickle spots,
Thanks for my nose,
Thanks for the wrinkles
I get on my toes.
Thanks for the songs
that I know how to sing,
Thank you, I think,
for my bathtub ring.

Suggestions for Going Further

1. Can children find all 8 words with *est* endings in the poem? Have them identify the root word in each case.
2. There is a lot of room for visual and geometric creativity here. Children can illustrate the existing poem. They can also make quilt patches of their own, use them to form a class quilt, and give positive descriptions of each other's patches using adjectives with *est* endings.
3. Discuss the opposites in the poem, such as biggest and smallest. Then give children a chance to add to the list of opposites in the poem. (E.g., *prettiest/ugliest, oldest/newest, plainest/fanciest.*)

Note: Since this poem has more lines than the Desktop Pocket Chart, the title strip has been designed to fit behind the first line.

Quilt Patches

Curled up
in my warmest patchwork quilt,
I choose the biggest,
    the smallest
    the lightest,
    the darkest,
    the cutest, the dullest,
and the grand champion
of all the patches!
Then snug in my quilt,
I fall into the deepest winter sleep.

contractions, ing

Suggestions for Going Further

1. Make sure children understand that the narrator of the poem is the mitten, and that *she* refers to the owner of the mitten. Ask children to find all the contractions and tell which two words they stand for. Then substitute *He's* for *She's* in the poem.
2. On the student poem or the poetry strips, cover most of line 3. (She's _____) Let children substitute a winter activity of their own (*throwing snowballs, making angels*).
3. Let children think of other verbs for lines 1 through 4 on the poetry strips. (E.g., *racing, tumbling, running, sliding,* and *slipping.*) Write the new verbs on sticky notes and try them out in the poem.

The Thoughts of a Winter Mitten

She's sliding on the driveway,
She's falling off her sled,
She's rolling down the hillside,
She's standing on her head.
She's lost me in a snow drift
and doesn't even see.
Until the season changes,
this snow is where I'll be.
Poor me!

Suggestions for Going Further

1. Brainstorm a list of animals and the places where they hibernate. (Bear and bat in a cave; turtle in a pond; ground squirrel, woodchuck, jumping mouse and skunk in a burrow in the ground.
2. Consider whiting out or taping over most of line 5 on the student poem. (But _____,). This enables children to interact with the poem by filling in the blank and illustrating their version of the poem.
3. On the poetry strips, highlight the blends in the poem with markers, Wikki Stix, or highlighting tape. Children can take turns reading the words and identifying the blends.
4. Make separate onset and rime cards for each word with a blend. Mix up the cards and let the children recreate the words.

Winter Play, Winter Sleep

We skate on the pond,
We play in the snow,
We sled on the hill,
Till spring winds blow.

But snake's in the ground,
And frog's in the lake.
In winter they sleep,
In spring they awake!

Suggestions for Going Further

1. Put the vowel pattern *oa* in the middle of a piece of chart paper and let children make a web using the *oa* words from the poem.

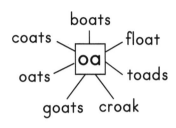

2. Create a blackline showing 100 raindrops on several children's raincoats. Let the children in your class use different methods to count the raindrops (grouping by tens, putting an X over raindrops that have been counted).

3. Have children create their own "100 pictures" and write sentences to describe them. (E.g., "I saw 100 stars in the sky.")

23

One Hundred

One hundred boats
float on the sea,
One hundred toads
croak by the tree,
One hundred goats
eat lots of oats,
How many raindrops
on our coats?

Suggestions for Going Further

1. Ask children for other rain images or activities. Some might be from a cold, rainy day, in contrast to the fun, rainy day in the poem.
2. You might want to white out the initial consonant or blend for each *ai* word in the student poem and let children fill in the blanks. (E.g., ___ain-bow) Alternatively, children could highlight the *ai* in each word with colored markers. Either way, the *ai* words will jump out from the page.
2. Start a list of words from the poem with the rime *ail*. Then brainstorm other words that belong on the list (*mail, trail, rail, nail, jail, pigtail, cottontail*).

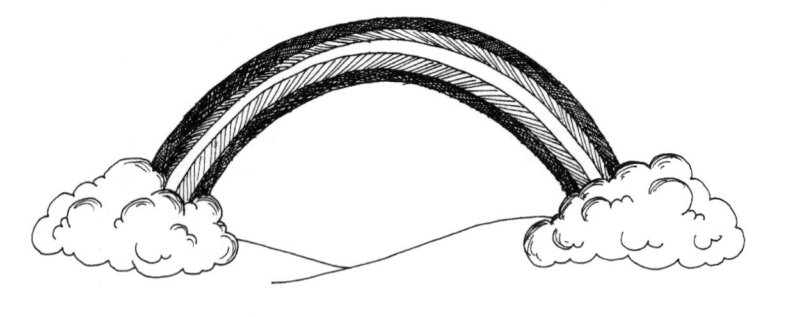

After the Rain

A rainbow paints the sky,
A leaf boat sails by.
A puppy shakes its tail,
Some raindrops in the pail.
A snail comes out to eat,
I'm wet from head to feet!

Suggestions for Going Further

1. Brainstorm vegetables other than tomatoes that could be grown in the garden. Try reading the poem with other veggies, or use white out or correction tape to create a blank in the student poem in place of the word *tomatoes*. Then children can fill in the blank with their favorite veggies. Alternatively, you could place sticky notes over the word *tomatoes* on the Desktop Pocket Chart and write in other veggies.

2. Help children find all the words in the poem with the diphthongs *ou* or *ow*. Create word cards, and have the children sort them by sound and spelling. Note that there are two sounds for *ow* in the poem. The first four lines contain words with one sound (*plow*) and the second four lines contain words with the other (*crow*). You might want to color code these two groups of words on the poetry strips, using markers, Wikki Stix, or highlighting tape.

Our Garden

We plow with our shovels,
Now time to plant seeds.
Tomatoes for us,
and flowers for bees.
When rows are all planted,
we'll make a scarecrow
to keep out the birds
so our garden can grow.

Suggestions for Going Further

1. Use sticky notes to cover the rhyming words on the poetry strips (*bed, pot, cat*). Children can complete the lines by studying the rhyming word from the previous line. For example, *Red* in line 2 rhymes with *bed* or *shed* in line 3. There are several options for completing each line.
2. Play with the opposites in the poem. Ask children what other kinds of bugs there could be. (*big/little, short/tall, nice/mean, sad/happy*). While you're at it, you might want to bring out some bug books and let children find bugs that fit the descriptions in the poem.

Bugs

Tan bugs,
Red bugs,
Resting on the bed bugs.
Cold bugs,
Hot bugs,
Hopping in the pot bugs.
Thin bugs,
Fat bugs,
Napping on the cat bugs!

Suggestions for Going Further

1. Brainstorm a list of possible occupations, and divide them into two groups, those having the *er* ending (e.g., *potters, lawyers, computer programmers*) and those without it (e.g., *accountant, psychologist, medical assistant*). Include the occupations in the poem.
2. Having children fill in the blank in the last line of the student poems will enable them to personalize the poem with their current "career plans." The results can be graphed into general categories such as athletes, artists, community helpers, and so on.
3. This poem could be used on Mothers' Day and/or Fathers' Day.
   Note: Since this poem has more lines than the Desktop Pocket Chart, the title strip has been designed to fit behind the first line.

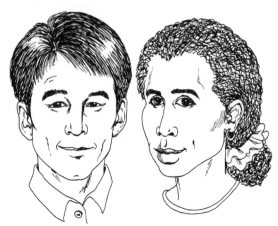

Mothers and Fathers

Some mothers are writers,
Some mothers are truckers,
Some mothers are workers
who help at the zoo.
Some fathers are drummers,
Some fathers are builders,
Some fathers are teachers
of me and of you.
When I am much bigger,
when I am much older,
I might be a _____ .
I'll love what I do!

Suggestions for Going Further

1. Have children search the poem for words that have a *y* ending. Don't forget *many*. Ask what sound the *y* makes in these words. Start a list of words with the *y* ending and add to it throughout the week (*Furry, heavy, merry, noisy, lucky, dusty, busy, spooky*).

2. This is a good time to allow children to write all the mixed feelings they may be having about the last days of school. After a brainstorming session, let them fill in the blanks for the frame:

   I'm _____.

   I'm _____.

   I'm _____.

   Alternatively, white out or tape over the words *ready* and *jumpy* in the student poem before copying it, and let children fill in new adjectives.

3. Discuss all the contractions in the poem. Try reading the poem using two words in place of each contraction and let children discover that the rhythm disappears.

The Last Days of School

I'm happy, I'm ready,
I'm silly, I'm sad.
I'm jolly, I'm jumpy,
I'm lazy, I'm glad.
I've got many feelings
cause school's almost done.
I'll miss many things,
but I know I'll have fun!

Suggestions for Going Further

1. Find all the rhyming words in the poem. Then write the rime *ay* in the center of a piece of chart paper and brainstorm a web of rhyming words from within the poem and from outside the poem.

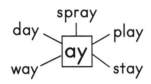

2. On the Desktop Pocket Chart, place a blank strip over most of line 5 (You can _____). Encourage children to create a replacement for line 6 by thinking up another sprinkler game and describing it (e.g., *pick up the sprinkler, sit on the spray, turn the water up and down*.) Note that the blank strip should be about 1" high.
Note: Since this poem has more lines than the Desktop Pocket Chart, the title strip has been designed to fit behind the first line.

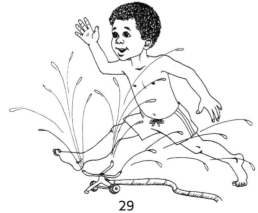

29

Running through the Sprinkler

You can let the water chase you,
You can jump across the spray.
When you're running
through the sprinkler,
there are lots of games to play.
You can stay there
as the water comes,
or run every-which-way,
When you're running
through the sprinkler
on a sunny summer day.

Suggestions for Going Further

1. To focus on the phoneme, have children highlight the long *a*/silent *e* words on their student poems. Or do so on the Desktop Pocket Chart using markers, Wikki Stix, or highlighting tape.
2. On chart paper, write these four rhymes: *ake, ate, ade, ale*. Then in a random fashion, say the long *a* words from the poem, as well as the following words: *lake, fake, take, late, hate, made, fade, trade, pale, male*. Have the children record each word where it belongs on the chart.
3. Work with the poem as a word problem. Decide on a price for each cake and lemonade. (The price for all items should be the same. 2¢ or 5¢ each works well.) Let children decide how many cakes and lemonades were sold. Have them draw a picture of the cakes and lemonades and figure out how much money was made in all.

The Sale

We had a sale
out in the shade,
with cakes we baked
and lemonade.
When we got hot,
we drank and ate,
and talked about
how much we'd made.

Suggestions for Going Further

1. Try whiting out or taping over the word *clouds* in line 7 of the student poem. Let children use their imaginations to fill in the blank. (Some possibilities are *trees, stars, sun, moon*, and *planets.*) Then lead a discussion about distances; for example, the sun is farther away than the clouds.
2. Make word cards to match the *p* words in the poem. Let children sort the cards into three categories: *p* at the beginning of the word, *p* at the end, and *p* at the beginning and end. Brainstorm other *p* words that fit into the three categories.

Swinging

I jump on the swing,
You give me a push.
I pump and I pump,
The air goes whoosh.

I pump and I pump,
I'm up past the park.
I'm up past the clouds,
I swing till it's dark.

Suggestions for Going Further

1. To make the poem interactive, white out or tape over the word *foxes* in line 4 before making copies of the student poem. Children can write another wild animal's name in the blank. (Some possibilities are *deer, bears, coyotes,* and *chipmunks.*)

2. The poem has a number of plural words with the ending *es.* Have children write them on word cards and sort the cards to find patterns. (The words can be sorted according to their root words, which end in *sh, ch, or x.*)

Camping

Picking up branches,
Lighting the matches.
Sitting on boxes,
Seeing some foxes.
Cooking the dinner,
Washing the dishes.
Watching the moon,
Sharing our wishes.

Suggestions for Going Further

1. This poem is very versatile because you can change the name of the animal to a name like Larry Lizard or Sammy Salamander. Thus, you have the freedom to focus on any beginning consonant sound. To do this, just white out or tape over the animal name on the student poem. Or create new animal names on word cards (1" high) and place them in the Desktop Pocket Chart. (Some possibilities are Betty Bunny, Connie Crab, Danny Dove, Freddy Frog, Georgy Gerbil, Gary Gekko, Holly Hamster, Jenny Jackrabbit, Kimmy Kitty, Larry Lizard, Molly Mouse, Polly Parrot, Queenie Quail, Sammy Salamander, Terry Turtle, Vinny Vole, Wanda Worm, and Zoey Zebra.)
2. On the Desktop Pocket Chart, write the names of other body parts on sticky notes or blank word cards. Substitute those body parts for the words *leg* or *neck* in the poem.
3. Pass out little plastic animals to the children so that they can act out the poem.

Nelly Newt

Nelly Newt
is on my leg,
Nelly Newt
is on my knee,
Nelly Newt
is on my neck,
Nelly thinks that I'm a tree!

Suggestions for Going Further

1. Provide a bag or two of twisted pretzels and let children create the pretzel alphabet. It's fun, instructive, and tasty. Note that it's better to slowly nibble away at part of the pretzel than to chomp down on it in one big bite. Sometimes it's easier to make a capital letter, and sometimes a lower-case. (Don't expect them to be perfect.)
2. Use the pretzel alphabet as the basis for reviewing the sounds of the consonants and vowels.
3. You can let each child pick a pretzel letter to glue down on paper and write a word starting with or including that letter.
   Note: Since this poem has more lines than the Desktop Pocket Chart, the title strip has been designed to fit behind the first line.

34

The Pretzel Alphabet

Think of a bag of pretzel treats
as a sculpture garden
ready to eat.

Nibble some here,
Nibble some there,
Bite off a curve
but do it with care.

Lay out the sculptures
for all to see,
Alphabet pretzels from A to Z.

Suggestions for Going Further

1. When using the poetry strips, consider covering the words *bat*, *cat*, and *hat* with sticky notes. Have children complete the poem by identifying these words through context clues and rhyming clues. Note that *cat* or *rat* would fit in line 3.
2. Let children use a pointer such as a Magic Wand to identify all the rhyming words in the poem. Point out the short *a* sound in each. Generate a bank of rhyming words with the rime *at*. Use words from the poem and words from outside the poem.
2. On the bottom of the student poem or on another paper, have children create and illustrate their own verse, using the following frame:

   When I _____,
   My shadow does that.

35

My Shadow

When I swing a bat,
My shadow does that.

When I pat a cat,
My shadow does that.

When I wear a hat,
My shadow does that.

My shadow is a copycat!

Suggestions for Going Further

1. Enjoy the silly surprises this poem has to offer, and list lots of other *janimals*. The activity can turn into a guessing game as children try to figure out which animal has become a *janimal*.
2. Let children illustrate one of the *janimals*. But make sure they include a J somewhere in the picture; for example, the J could be a tail.
3. The poem offers an interesting way to focus on any beginning consonant sound. Try some others. For example, you could brainstorm *banimals* such as babbits, bostriches, and bimpanzees, or *zanimals* such as zalligators, zippos, and zeopards.

Janimals

Jocodiles, juffaloes,

vampire jats.

Jutterflies, jizards,

Australian jombats.

Joosters and joodpeckers,

spotted jobcats.

Billy joats, jamsters,

and don't forget jats!

Suggestions for Going Further

1. Before copying the student poem, you can white out or tape over the word *teddy* or *pencil*. Children can personalize the poem by writing in a possession that they often lose in their rooms.
2. Using the poem, make word cards of the words with the rimes *ess, et,* and *est*. After letting children sort the cards, read the following words out of order, and have children decide which category they belong in: *pet, let, bet, met, wet, net, test, pest, rest, less, chess, bless, press*.
3. Alternatively, let children use sets of letters to create words containing the three rimes. The Word Builder Kit can be useful here.

Messy Room

A room that's all messy
is not always best.

I can't find my teddy,
You can't find your vest.

I can't find my pencil,
You can't find your dress.

Get ready, get set,
Let's clean up this mess!

Suggestions for Going Further

1. There are two ways that children can easily personalize the poem. First, they can fill in the last line with the name of a friend. Second, they can complete the frame:

    When I get sick,
    I _____.
    When I get sick,
    I _____.

2. Ask children to search the poem for short *i* words, and make a list to chant together.
3. Generate a web of rhyming words using the rime *ick*, which is one of the most common rhymes.

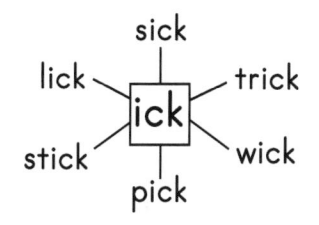

Sick

When I get sick,
it's pretty icky.
My lips are dry,
My nose is drippy.
I sip and sip
and eat a bit,
But even if I rest all day,
_____ can't come in
and play.

Suggestions for Going Further

1. Have children build the poem by placing a number less than 10 in the blank in line 5. Children can follow through by acting out the poem with a pot of real popcorn, with manipulatives, or with popcorn cut from index tag and placed in the Desktop Pocket Chart. No matter which method is used, children can write a number sentence to match the poem. (E.g., 10 - 6 = 4)
2. Use chart paper to create webs of rhyming words with the rimes *ot* and *op*. Alternatively, let children use sets of letters to build words with these two rimes. Use Word Builder Kits if you have them.

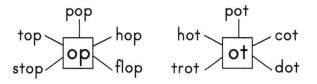

Popping Popcorn

Ten little popcorns
sitting in the pot.
The pot gets hot,
and the popcorns pop.
_____ little popcorns
hop from the pot.

On a Good Morning

The sky is blue,
There's lots to do.

I'm getting fed
while still in bed.

My hair lies flat,
I'm glad of that.

My homework's done
and it was fun.

On time for school,
My life is cool.

One of Those Mornings

I wake up mad,
The weather's bad.

The room is hot,
The toast is not.

My hair sticks up,
There's no clean cup.

My homework's wrong,
It took too long.

I'm late today.
What can I say?

Suggestions for Going Further

1. The two poems are companion poems; the sub-jects covered in each poem are the same. Ask children what kind of morning they are having. On their student poems, have them illustrate a verse or two that they can relate to. Or have them add a verse and illustrate it. Their verses don't have to rhyme. Possible topics are siblings, bag lunches, backpacks, shoes, clothes, bikes, and bike hel-mets.
2. Have children hunt for and sort all the short vowel words in the poem.
3. On the poetry strips, cover one of the rhyming words in each verse with a sticky note, and ask children to identify it.

   Note: Since these poems have more lines than the Desktop Pocket Chart, the title strips have been designed to fit behind the first line.

On a Good Morning
and One of Those Mornings
can be found on page 40.

Suggestions for Going Further

1. Before copying the student poem, consider creating a blank in place of the word *white* in the last line. Then children can write in a color and illustrate the poem accordingly. Alternatively, for an especially fun activity, have children complete and illustrate the poetry frame below. Children can write a gooey substance in the first blank and the appropriate color in the last blank.

> The pup sees *jelly*,
> The pup falls down.
> The pup has turned
> from white to *purple*.

2. With the poetry strips in the Desktop Pocket Chart, have children underline or highlight the short *u* words with marker, Wikki Stix, or highlighting tape.
3. On chart paper, write the following rimes at the tops of three columns: *_un, _up, _ud*. Say words from the poem, and from outside the poem, that fit in one of the columns. Have children write the words in the correct list on the chart paper.

Funny Pup

The funny pup is having fun.
She runs and jumps
out in the sun.
The pup sees mud,
The pup falls down.
The pup has turned
from white to brown.

Suggestions for Going Further

1. It's easy to make this poem interactive. Before making copies of the student poem, just tape over or white out the word *carrots*, and let children write in crunchy foods they eat, such as chips, celery, apples, and crackers.
2. On the Desktop Pocket Chart, you can highlight all the *ch* words with marker, Wikki Stix, or highlighting tape. Then the poem can be chanted with the crunchy, munchy *ch* sounds emphasized.
3. Since all but one of the *ch* digraphs appear at the ends of words, it might be useful to brainstorm *ch* words with the digraph in the initial position. If food words appear on the list, decide if they are crunchy or not (e.g., *chicken, chips, cheese, cherries, Cheerios, chili*).

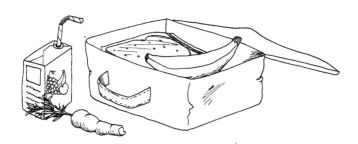

Lunch

I crunch, I munch,
I chew a bunch of carrots
when I eat my lunch.

And when I've munched
on all my lunch,
I wash it down
with cold fruit punch.

So what's to munch
inside your lunch?

Suggestions for Going Further

1. Children can make the poem their own by substituting words for *shorts* and/or *shirt*. Just white out or tape over the word(s) on the student poem before copying it.
2. Note that the poem could be about a child rushing off to a variety of activities. Children can decide where the child is going and write in appropriate words when replacing the words *shorts* and/or *shirt*. (Some possibilities are *shinguards, party dress, bathing suit,* and *baseball pants.*)
3. Make word cards from the 8 *sh* words in the poem. Let the children help you generate a list of other pieces of clothing that include the *sh* digraph (*T-shirt, undershirt, shinguards, shades*).
4. Sort the cards in different ways. (Where is the *sh* in the word? Is the word a thing or an action? How many letters are in the word?)

Late!

I pull on my shorts,
I pull on my shirt.

My shoes go on last,
I pull them on fast.

I brush all my teeth,
I wash in a flash.

Then out the front door,
I rush in a dash!

Suggestions for Going Further

1. Let children brainstorm different endings for line 2: and it's hard to _____. (*eat apples, eat corn, whistle, blow bubbles*) Use several of the children's suggestions in the Desktop Pocket Chart poem by handwriting them on blank word strips and placing them in the poem. Note that strips need to be about 1" high.
2. Have children find all the words with the *th* digraph in the poem. Make two lists of the words, those that begin with *th* and those that end with *th*. Then read the following words out of order and ask children which list to record them on: *bath, path, math, booth, moth, cloth, sloth, north, south, thin, thick, thud, thank, thing, then, that, them*. Note that *th* has two different sounds, as in the words *thin* and *this*.

Loose Tooth

I have this loose tooth,
and it's hard to chew gum.
I wiggle this tooth
back and forth
with my thumb.
The tooth is on top,
Soon out it will come.
With the Tooth Fairy's gift,
I think I'll buy gum!

wh

Suggestions for Going Further

1. When reading this poem with the children, point out the question marks and read with inflection.
2. Let children bring in a favorite stuffed animal toy and answer the questions posed in the poem. This can be done at the bottom of the page, or you can draw lines at the end of each line of poetry before copying the student poem. Graphs can be made from the results.
3. On the Desktop Pocket Chart, highlight the *wh* words using marker, Wikki Stix, or highlighting tape. Ask children: Where do most of the *wh* words appear in the sentences? (the beginning) What other "question words" are there? (*Why? Where? Whose?*) Why would a stuffed whale fit in nicely with this poem? (*Whale* has the digraph *wh*.)

Which Toy?

What's your favorite
stuffed animal toy?
Is it a girl?
Or is it a boy?
What is its name?
Is it white, brown, or blue?
When did you get it?
Who gave it to you?

Suggestions for Going Further

1. Let each child personalize the poem by writing her or his favorite recess activity in the blank in the student poem.
2. Brainstorm other activities with balls (*passing, batting, punting, bouncing, catching, pitching*). Place sticky notes over the word *throwing* on the poetry strips, and try some of these other words in its place.
2. Let children inspect each *ing* word to find the root word. For some root words, the last letter has been doubled. Which ones?
4. Act out the poem.

47

Playing at Recess

There's running and skipping and hopping and jumping.

There's shooting and throwing and kicking a ball.

There's climbing and hanging and flipping and swinging.

But _____ is what I do best of them all.

Suggestions for Going Further

1. Make lists of rimes as shown below. Let children use words from the poem and other words from outside the poem to fill in the onsets.

__ome	__one	__oke
__ome	__one	__oke
__ome	__one	__oke

2. Children love to recount accidents and injuries. Let them complete the following frame:

   I _____.
   I hurt _____.
   Example:
   I fell off my bike on a bumpy road.
   I hurt my knee.

3. Each child will have a favorite ice cream flavor for line 7. These can be organized on a bar graph.
   Note: Since this poem has more lines than the Desktop Pocket Chart, the title strip has been designed to fit behind the first line.

Broken Bone

I fell down hard
and broke a bone.
I got a cast
and went back home.
Dad read me books
and told me jokes.
I ate a chocolate
ice cream cone.
(It's not so bad
to break a bone!)

contractions

Suggestions for Going Further

1. Talk about activities and rules at home that children would rather do without, such as cleaning rooms, setting the table, and taking out garbage. Using blank strips, substitute some of these activities for *taking baths* in line 7 of the poetry strips. Strips should be about 6" long and 1" high.
2. Let children find all the contractions in the poem and help you write out the two words they stand for. Point out *is not* in the last line of the poem, and have children figure out what contraction could be made from the two words.

I Won't

I can't!
I won't!
I'll scream and cry,
I'll yell and whine,
I don't see why
you don't agree
that taking baths
is not for me!

Suggestions for Going Further

1. Have children highlight the long e words in the poem: *Pete, these, here's, me, he, be, three, see,* and *deal*. Do this on the poetry strips as well.
2. Create word cards for the long e words. You might want to add the following words as well: *Eve, Steve, Cleve, athlete, compete, seal*. Then children can sort the cards into four categories: e e, e, ee, ea.
3. Be mathematicians. On the Desktop Pocket Chart, place sticky notes over the numbers in lines 3 and 4 and write in new numbers. (E.g., When he is 8, I will be 9. When he is 60, I will be 61.) Or change lines 2, 3, and 4. (E.g., Line 2 could be: When he was 1, I was 3.)

Pete and Me

I'm older than my brother Pete,
When he was two, I was three.
When he is six, I will be seven,
When he is ten, I'll be eleven.
Now here's the deal
with Pete and me.
Take all these numbers
and you'll see,
The older one is always me!

Suggestions for Going Further

1. Help children find all the long *u* words in the poem.
2. With musical instruments from the classroom, act out the poem as you recite it. Have children on rhythm instruments beat the rhythm of the poem.

Super Duper Band

The mule plays drums,
The sheep plays flute.
The pig plays sax,
He thinks he's cute.
The bird's the boss,
She sings the tune.
The dog just howls
at the moon.

Suggestions for Going Further

1. On the bottom of the student poem sheet, let children complete the following frame and draw a picture of the parade.

   I'd like to _____

   in the parade.

2. On the poetry strips, let children point out words with a long vowel and silent *e*. Record the words on lists according to vowel sound. (*parade, wave*) (*these*) (*time, ride, like, bikes, white*) (*hope*) (*huge, flute*).

3. Act out the poem, especially if it's near May Day.

Parade Time

We hope you'll be in our parade.

Here's what we like to do:

We play the flute

or wave these flags

of red and white and blue.

We ride our bikes or walk our dogs

or hold a huge balloon.

We hope you'll be in our parade

and bring a pal or two.

Suggestions for Going Further

1. Before making copies of the student poem, white out or tape over the *ea* in the appropriate words. This will make the poem into a "puzzle" for children to complete.
2. The children can then help you compile a master list of all the *ea* and *ai* words in the poem.
3. Have children write and illustrate their own "My Dream" poems. You might want to talk about the two meanings of the word *dream*. In conjunction with Martin Luther King, Jr. Day, children could have the option of writing about dreams as in "hopes and dreams." Note that sometimes we dream at night about our hopes and dreams.

My Dream

I mailed a leaf,

I sailed to sea.

I ate a hot meal

of oatmeal and tea.

I painted a sunbeam,

I trained a small flea.

The dream that I dreamed

seemed as real as could be.

Numbers, Quote Marks, long i

Suggestions for Going Further

1. Let children find all the number words in the poem. Then make a complete list of the number words from *one* to *ten*.
2. Be problem solvers. Have children use manipulatives and/or draw pictures to show how many mice would be in each cage if there were five cages, or if there were six cages.
3. Ask children to find 8 words with long *i* and silent *i* in the poem. Help them enjoy the sound of all the long *i* words in the first line.

Two White Mice Were Nice

Two white mice were nice
till they had babies twice.
With five or six cages,
it got quite outrageous.
My mother said, "Hey!
Thirty mice cannot stay.
One tiny white mouse
is enough for one house!"

Suggestions for Going Further

1. To make the poem interactive, create a blank in the poem where the word *jacket* appears in lines 1 and 7. Children can personalize the poem by writing in some item they've lost in the past. Use the names of these items to create a class graph of *Things We've Lost*.

2. The poem includes words in which the *st* blend is the initial sound and words in which it is the final sound. On the student poems, children can underline these two sets of words with different-colored markers. On the Desktop Pocket Chart, the words can also be highlighted using two colors.

3. Start two or three lists of *st* words and add to them throughout the week. The lists could be words that start with *st*, words in which the *st* is last, and words such as *blister* and *mister*, in which the *st* is in the middle of the word.

Lost and Found

I lost my best jacket,
It's nowhere around.
I stop and I look
in the Lost and Found.

There's lots of lost stuff,
I look through it fast.
Oh, there's my best jacket,
I've found it at last!

Poetry Strip Contents

Note: Due to the requirements of our printer, the page numbers
appear on the bottom strip on each page. To avoid confusion,
we recommend that you make one copy and white out the
page number before copying the poetry strips onto card stock.

New School Year

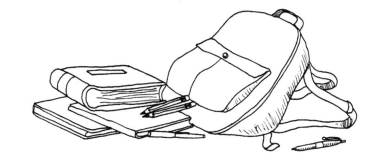

New room,

New pens,

New books,

New friends.

New packs,

New year,

New class,

Let's cheer!

Nice and Friendly

I say hi to Rosa,

Rosa says hi to Lan,

Lan says hi to Bo,

and Bo says hi to Don.

6 When I feel nice and friendly,

7 I like to pass it on.

8 _____ says hi to _____

1 We All Need Friends

2 "Hi," "Hello,"

3 "Come play with me."

4 These are friendly words, you see.

⁵ To be a friend

⁶ can take awhile,

⁷ yet it can start with just a smile.

⁸ I need a friend.

⁹ to play with me.

¹⁰ I'll be your friend if you agree.

¹ Coming to School

2 I come by bus,

3 Mike comes by trike.

4 Some people drive,

5 and some people hike.

6 Spike likes to run,

7 Ike likes to bike.

8 The ways that we come

9 aren't always alike.

You are Special

What is your name

and your favorite game?

What do you like

and what can you do?

What can you teach us

7 that's silly or new?

8 So many things

9 we wish that we knew.

10 Yet what makes you special

11 is just being you.

1

A Tree Has Arms

2 A tree has arms

3 but has no legs.

4 It cannot run around.

5 But in the fall,

6 it wears a gown

7 of yellow, orange, and brown.

1 Apples in Autumn

It's hard to eat apples

without my front teeth,

But apples in autumn

are really a treat.

The apples are squooshy

down under my feet,

But those from the tree

are still crunchy and sweet!

Backpacks

My backpack is white,

Your backpack is black.

My backpack's so full,

it's hard to unpack.

Your backpack is heavy,

My backpack is light.

8 It's smack on my back,

9 It rides piggyback.

1 I'm Thankful

2 Thanks for my tickle spots,

3 Thanks for my nose,

4 Thanks for the wrinkles

5 I get on my toes.

⁶ Thanks for the songs

⁷ that I know how to sing,

⁸ Thank you, I think, for my bathtub ring.

¹

Quilt Patches

² Curled up

³ in my warmest patchwork quilt,

4 I choose the biggest,

5 the smallest

6 the lightest,

7 the darkest,

8 the cutest, the dullest,

9 and the grand champion of all the patches!

10 Then snug in my quilt,

11 I fall into the deepest winter sleep.

The Thoughts of a Winter Mitten

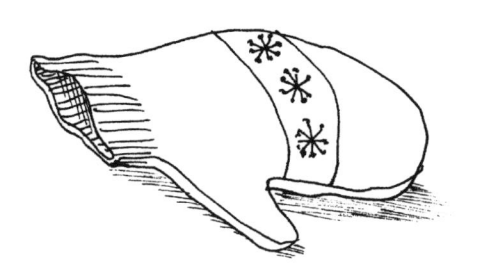

She's sliding on the driveway,

She's falling off her sled,

She's rolling down the hillside,

She's standing on her head.

She's lost me in a snow drift

and doesn't even see.

8 Until the season changes,

9 this snow is where I'll be.

10 Poor me!

1 Winter Play,
   Winter Sleep

2 We skate on the pond,

3 We play in the snow,

4 We sled on the hill,

71

5 Till spring winds blow.

6 But snake's in the ground,

7 And frog's in the lake.

8 In winter they sleep,

9 In spring they awake!

1 One Hundred

2 One hundred boats

3 float on the sea,

4 One hundred toads

5 croak by the tree,

6 One hundred goats

7 eat lots of oats,

8 How many raindrops

9 on our coats?

After the Rain

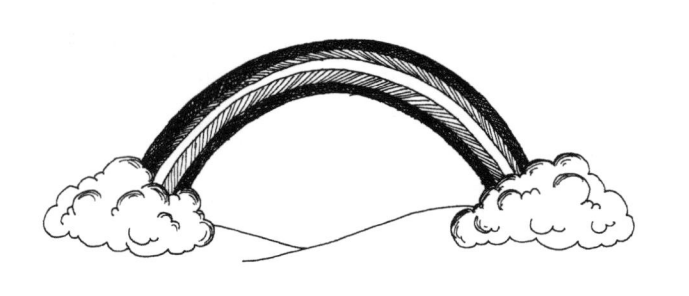

A rainbow paints the sky,

A leaf boat sails by.

A puppy shakes its tail,

Some raindrops in the pail.

A snail comes out to eat,

I'm wet from head to feet!

Our Garden

We plow with our shovels,

Now time to plant seeds.

Tomatoes for us,

and flowers for bees.

When rows are all planted,

we'll make a scarecrow

to keep out the birds

so our garden can grow.

1
Bugs

2
Tan bugs,

3
Red bugs,

4
Resting on the bed bugs.

5
Cold bugs,

6 Hot bugs,

7 Hopping in the pot bugs.

8 Thin bugs,

9 Fat bugs,

10 Napping on the cat bugs!

1 Mothers and Fathers

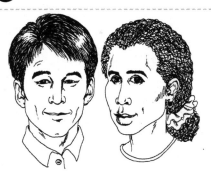

2 Some mothers are writers,

3 Some mothers are truckers,

4 Some mothers are workers

5 who help at the zoo.

6 Some fathers are drummers,

7 Some fathers are builders,

8 Some fathers are teachers of me and of you.

9 When I am much bigger,

¹⁰ when I am much older,

¹¹ I might be a _____. I'll love what I do!

¹ # The Last Days of School

² I'm happy, I'm ready,

³ I'm silly, I'm sad.

⁴ I'm jolly, I'm jumpy,

⁵ I'm lazy, I'm glad.

6 I've got many feelings

7 cause school's almost done.

8 I'll miss many things,

9 but I know I'll have fun!

1 Running through the Sprinkler

2 You can let the water chase you,

3 You can jump across the spray.

⁴ When you're running

⁵ through the sprinkler,

⁶ there are lots of games to play.

⁷ You can stay there as the water comes,

⁸ or run every-which-way,

⁹ When you're running

¹⁰ through the sprinkler

¹¹ on a sunny summer day.

The Sale

We had a sale

out in the shade,

with cakes we baked

and lemonade.

When we got hot,

we drank and ate,

⁸ and talked about

⁹ how much we'd made.

¹ Swinging

² I jump on the swing,

³ You give me a push.

⁴ I pump and I pump,

⁵ The air goes whoosh.

6 I pump and I pump,

7 I'm up past the park.

8 I'm up past the clouds,

9 I swing till it's dark.

1 Camping

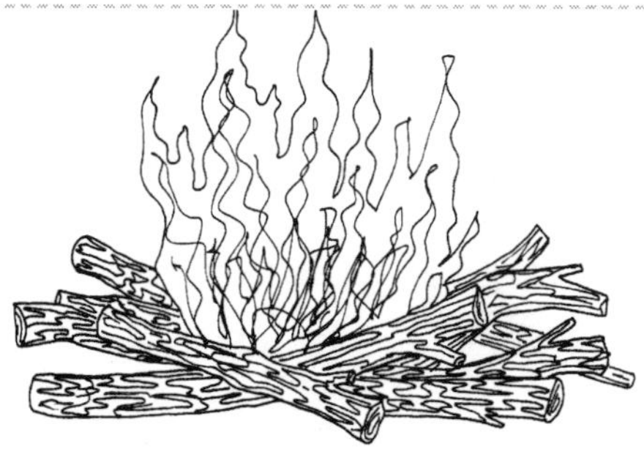

2 Picking up branches,

3 Lighting the matches.

4 Sitting on boxes,

5 Seeing some foxes.

6 Cooking the dinner,

7 Washing the dishes.

8 Watching the moon,

9 Sharing our wishes.

1 Nelly Newt

2 Nelly Newt

3 is on my leg,

4 Nelly Newt

5 is on my knee,

6 Nelly Newt

7 is on my neck,

8 Nelly thinks that I'm a tree!

The Pretzel Alphabet

Think of a bag of pretzel treats

as a sculpture garden

ready to eat.

Nibble some here, Nibble some there,

Bite off a curve

but do it with care.

⁸ Lay out the sculptures for all to see,

⁹ Alphabet pretzels

¹⁰ from A to Z.

¹ My Shadow

² When I swing a bat,

³ My shadow does that.

⁴ When I pat a cat,

My shadow does that.

When I wear a hat,

My shadow does that.

My shadow is a copycat!

Janimals

Jocodiles, juffaloes,

vampire jats.

Jutterflies, jizards,

Australian jombats.

Joosters and joodpeckers,

spotted jobcats.

Billy joats, jamsters,

and don't forget jats!

Messy Room

2 A room that's all messy

3 is not always best.

4 I can't find my teddy,

5 You can't find your vest.

6 I can't find my pencil,

7 You can't find your dress.

8 Get ready, get set,

9 Let's clean up this mess!

Sick

When I get sick,

it's pretty icky.

My lips are dry,

My nose is drippy.

I sip and sip

and eat a bit,

8 But even if I rest all day,

9 _____ can't come in

10 and play.

1   Popping Popcorn

2 Ten little popcorns

3 sitting in the pot.

4 The pot gets hot,

5 and the popcorns pop.

6 _____ little popcorns

7 hop from the pot.

1
On a
Good
Morning

One of
Those
Mornings

2 The sky is blue,

I wake up mad,

3 There's lots to do.

The weather's bad.

4 I'm getting fed	The room is hot,
5 while still in bed.	The toast is not.
6 My hair lies flat,	My hair sticks up,
7 I'm glad of that.	There's no clean cup.
8 My homework's done	My homework's wrong,
9 and it was fun.	It took too long.
10 On time for school,	I'm late today.
11 My life is cool.	What can I say?

Funny Pup

The funny pup is having fun.

She runs and jumps

out in the sun.

The pup sees mud,

The pup falls down.

The pup has turned

⁸ from white to brown.

¹ Lunch

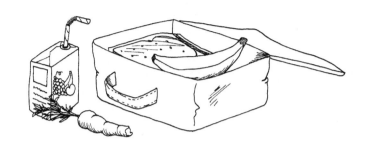

² I crunch, I munch,

³ I chew a bunch of carrots

⁴ when I eat my lunch.

⁵ And when I've munched

⁶ on all my lunch,

97

7 I wash it down

8 with cold fruit punch.

9 So what's to munch

10 inside your lunch?

1 Late!

2 I pull on my shorts,

3 I pull on my shirt.

4 My shoes go on last,

5 I pull them on fast.

6 I brush all my teeth,

7 I wash in a flash.

8 Then out the front door,

9 I rush in a dash!

1 Loose Tooth

I have this loose tooth,
and it's hard to chew gum.
I wiggle this tooth
back and forth with my thumb.
The tooth is on top,
Soon out it will come.
With the Tooth Fairy's gift,
I think I'll buy gum!

Which Toy?

What's your favorite

stuffed animal toy?

Is it a girl?

Or is it a boy?

What is its name?

Is it white, brown, or blue?

8 When did you get it?

9 Who gave it to you?

1 Playing at Recess

2 There's running and skipping

3 and hopping and jumping.

4 There's shooting and throwing

5 and kicking a ball.

6 There's climbing and hanging

7 and flipping and swinging.

8 But _____ is what

9 I do best of them all.

1 Broken Bone

2 I fell down hard

3 and broke a bone.

I got a cast

and went back home.

Dad read me books

and told me jokes.

I ate a chocolate ice cream cone.

(It's not so bad to break a bone!)

I Won't

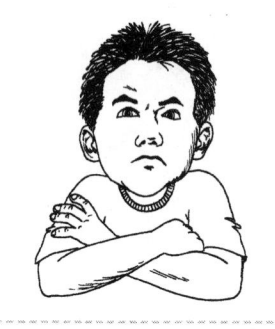

2 I can't!

3 I won't!

4 I'll scream and cry,

5 I'll yell and whine,

6 I don't see why

7 you don't agree

8 that taking baths

9 is not for me!

Pete and Me

I'm older than my brother Pete,

When he was two, I was three.

When he is six, I will be seven,

When he is ten, I'll be eleven.

Now here's the deal

with Pete and me.

8 Take all these numbers

9 and you'll see,

10 The older one is always me!

1 Super Duper Band

2 The mule plays drums,

3 The sheep plays flute.

4 The pig plays sax,

107

5 He thinks he's cute.

6 The bird's the boss,

7 She sings the tune.

8 The dog just howls at the moon.

I

Parade Time

2 We hope you'll be in our parade.

3 Here's what we like to do:

4 We play the flute

5 or wave these flags

6 of red and white and blue.

7 We ride our bikes

8 or walk our dogs

9 or hold a huge balloon.

10 We hope you'll be in our parade

and bring a pal or two.

My Dream

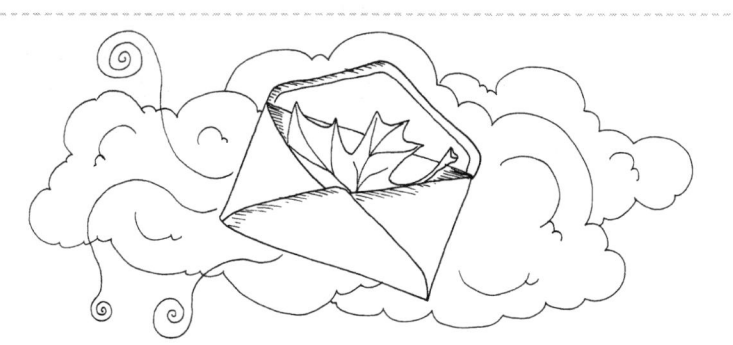

I mailed a leaf,

I sailed to sea.

I ate a hot meal

of oatmeal and tea.

I painted a sunbeam,

⁷ I trained a small flea.

⁸ The dream that I dreamed

⁹ seemed as real as could be.

¹ Two White Mice
Were Nice

² Two white mice were nice

³ till they had babies twice.

⁴ With five or six cages,

5 it got quite outrageous.

6 My mother said, "Hey!

7 Thirty mice cannot stay.

8 One tiny white mouse

9 is enough for one house!"

1 Lost and Found

2 I lost my best jacket,

3 It's nowhere around.

4 I stop and I look

5 in the Lost and Found.

6 There's lots of lost stuff,

7 I look through it fast.

8 Oh, there's my best jacket,

9 I've found it at last!

9

10

11

12

Notes

Seasonal Poems and Phonics, Too!

Notes